...But God

From PAIN to PURPOSE

SHARON GILMORE
with
VICTORIA HOLMES

XULON PRESS

Xulon Press
2301 Lucien Way #415
Maitland, FL 32751
407.339.4217
www.xulonpress.com

© 2018 by Sharon Gilmore

All rights reserved solely by the author. The author guarantees all contents are original and do not infringe upon the legal rights of any other person or work. No part of this book may be reproduced in any form without the permission of the author. The views expressed in this book are not necessarily those of the publisher.

Unless otherwise indicated, Scripture quotations taken from the New King James Version (NKJV). Copyright © 1982 by Thomas Nelson, Inc. Used by permission. All rights reserved.

Printed in the United States of America.

ISBN-13: 9781545628102

DEDICATION

I dedicate this book to my husband, Samuel Gilmore! You are my Hero, my King, and the man that chooses to love me unconditionally. Thank you, for deciding to be a father at 20 years old! I appreciate you for who you are! We have had ups and downs, through it all we are still standing. I love you more today than I ever have. The father you are to our children is invaluable, the friend you are to me is irreplaceable, and the visionary you are for this family will establish our legacy! I am proud to be Mrs. Gilmore.

To my children, each of you has taught me countless life-lessons; and I am a better version of me because of you. My Only Begotten Son [Alex], you are the most determined person I know, you will have everything you set your mind to obtain. I'm so proud of the man you are and the father you will be. My Overachiever [Faith], I yearned to be a better woman because of you! Your dreams will come true because you possess the spirit of excellence and epitomize the meaning of diligence. Nothing is beyond you! My Boss Lady [Grace], you are the promise! Your life has compelled me to believe God, no matter what! You embody boldness, love, and joy simultaneously! I don't know what you will choose to be, but I do know you will slay it!

To my spiritual God-parents and marital mentors, Ross & Evelyn Edwards, I love you eternally! My parents were gone, but you were there to love me and guide me. My marriage has survived and thrived because of your commitment to seeing us through it all. I love and appreciate you!

TABLE OF CONTENTS

Foreword... ix
Preface.. xi

Chapter 1:   Daddy Issues 1
Chapter 2:   I am Lois' Daughter.................. 9
Chapter 3:   Innocence Lost 16
Chapter 4:   The Burden of being The Only 20
Chapter 5:   Welcome to Hollywood 25
Chapter 6:   I'm Addicted........................ 30
Chapter 7:   Prison & Promotion 34
Chapter 8:   Laid to Rest 41
Chapter 9:   Single & A Mother 46
Chapter 10: The Best: Samuel Gilmore 52
Chapter 11: The Promise 61
Chapter 12: Promise Problems.................... 68
Chapter 13: Purpose & Destiny................... 77

FOREWORD

The connection between Sharon and I is undoubtedly divine. Some relationships seemingly occur by happenstance, while others are strategically ordained. The joining of Sharon and I is fated, and I thank God for her. We were introduced to each other by a mutual friend. The magnetism of our individual purposes established the mutual purpose of our relationship! I felt liberated in doing what I do best… I am an editor, a writer, an author, and a gifted literary enhancer.

Sharon invited me to her journey, and we both allowed God to guide us in the way that we should go. Sharon helped me realize that when God chooses us… He is intentional! God never does a work without knowing it will glorify Him and be glorified! Sharon intuitively sensed that I was intentionally hiding! Not in the sense of ducking and dodging... but in my deliberate acceptance of remaining in the background.

Sharon Gilmore said, "No more hiding, come to the forefront and do not linger in the background any longer. We need each other, you will help me co-author this memoir!" In that instance, I experienced a "But God" moment! Elevation and acceleration come when we acknowledge and accept our NEED of God... and at that moment, we give way to God's provision. So, when people wonder "how and why" the only explanation that can be rendered... is God!

> ...But God is the explanation for the unexplainable! Allow this memoir to bless and propel your life into complete dependence on God!

Victoria Holmes
Literary Coach/Editorial Expert
Literary Impressions LLC

PREFACE

I dreamt of being an author, after an encounter with God. One day I heard, "You are a bestselling author." I said, "Really God," and suddenly He reminded me of how I loved writing. God released my heart's desire although I was unaware of how powerful my God-given gift is! Over the next three years, I meditated on the book, and God revealed its title and the purpose.

Momentarily, I believed my self-doubt more than I trusted God. The attack began in my mind, and "it" tried to keep me in my past… but God immediately quickened me! Fortunately, at that moment I realized "my now" and "my past" work together to propel me towards my future. So, I could not be dismayed about who I was…but I had to rejoice in who I am! This mindset catapulted the production and the revelation of my first book. I struggled with the challenge of trying to produce what I heard God say and the instruction God gave me to "speak the book". I could not understand how to speak it. Literally, I was introduced to an unconventional method of completing a book. I spoke the book into my phone over the course of three days. It was unreal, it was simplistic, and it was exactly what God said, who would have known...But God!

> And they overcame him by the blood of the Lamb and by the word of their testimony, and they did not love their lives to the death.
> Revelations 12:11 NKJV

~Sharon Gilmore~

Chapter One:

DADDY ISSUES

I couldn't help but imagine a distraught twelve year old boy; his parents killed in a house fire an erased identity and a new adopted family with different values and beliefs systems. I wondered who my father was before this...

In 1964, my father was drafted into the military for the Vietnam War, and he decided to marry my mother out of fear of possibly dying without someone who would identify him as a family member. He needed a comfortable personally-established connection. Conceptually, I understand his rationale, and the reality of his past affected every decision he made. So, my father's need for belonging was warranted, as well as the lingering heartache and the brokenness...

My father endured the Vietnam War and returned home after four years. Although he came home alive, he was accompanied by PTSD. Unfortunately, during this time the ignorance of PTSD meant that the illness was nonexistent. The soldiers were brought home and released to their families; they (the veterans) returned changed forever by the experiences of death, loss, fear, and the looming expectation of being strong and unscathed. Alcohol and drunkenness became the periodic coping mechanism for my father when life overwhelmed him.

I learned of my father's veteran status when I was seven years old; I found his military pins one day while snooping through my mother's closet. My eyes glistened in amazement, and I thought to myself "Daddy was in the military?" "Why don't we talk about it..." as I look back I don't remember my family ever acknowledging his service and this broke my heart. As I got older, I understood who my father is and what he accomplished; I now understand not being acknowledged by his family intensified his brokenness.

My parents' marriage didn't start as a fairytale romance and was unconventional in every aspect of the idea. I can only imagine what they felt upon my dad's return to a marriage they did not expect to last beyond the war.

Nevertheless, divorce was not an option. Neither of them had seen a successful marriage and their challenges were inevitable–how could they emulate something their comprehension was unable to grasp. It was there opportunity to change the course their lineage, starting with remaining married. Over the tenure of their marriage, they overcame obstacles that should have destroyed their union, but they remained married. Their five children served as the evidence of their commitment. However, it was during their separation that my parents came to the knowledge of God and their marriage was strengthened.

When my father moved into our home I was extremely excited. Prior to my daddy's arrival, my mother instructed us to obey him and to do as we were told. She ensured that we respected and revered him as the man of the house. My brothers had embraced that role, but everything was about to change! I could sense from my brothers' reactions that this was not their first experience living with daddy; they had seen and experienced a side of him I had yet to experience because I was the "baby girl."

My father moved in and inevitably I learned things about him that I didn't know before. He was a self-taught auto mechanic, an extremely hard-worker, reserved, quiet, and outwardly he always seemed evenly-tempered. He was debonair and sophisticated. My father always smelled good and the scent of his embrace lingered even when he was no longer present. I loved that about him!

Day in and day out my father simply existed in our home. I cannot recall memories of family vacations, deep conversations, daddy-daughter dates, or anything remotely close to the fatherly bond I desired. This caused an internal brokenness for me because the one man that intrigued me most apparently had no desire to connect with me.

Every little girl looks at her father in admiration and has a desperate yearning to know him, and I didn't receive that. When he was away due to war drafting his absence was explainable, but his absent-presence when he returned was unfathomable for me. I did not and could not understand his emotional detachment from our family.

My father worked from sunrise to sunset, and when he returned home he isolated himself in his room until it was time for dinner. We sat and ate in silence. We were told not to talk at the dinner table, I didn't understand why. It seemed like the logical place to discuss our thoughts. I watched sitcoms like The Cosby Show and Fresh Prince of Bel Air; they looked like us and they always talked during dinner. I had a deep desire to sit at the table and talk; this was the first time I felt constrained... unable to do something that felt natural to me and it was prohibited by my daddy.

My anxieties skyrocketed due to my father's controlling antics, I felt bound! When my father no longer allowed me to wear pants, I wanted him gone. My father insisted that girls should always wear dresses, and I preferred pants or shorts. I wasn't the girly girl he wanted, and I hated that my father treated me as if I was not good enough .I simply wanted to be accepted and embraced by the one man who should have loved me automatically and unconditionally.

Thus, the onset of my "daddy-issues" ensued, and a wedge of distance occurred between us. Although I had a yearning to be close to him, I became conflicted with who my father was and who I wanted him to be. At this point, my rebellion against him was steadily brewing. I wanted to launch a war against him, all by myself. His idea of being a lady meant to be quietly subdued; and by nature, I exist on the other end of the spectrum – PROUD and LOUD! I was loud as a little girl and my father constantly tried to apprehend me. His controlling presence made me feel inadequate.

My pursuit of acceptance and liberty began. As a middle-schooler, I sought the attention of anyone who acted interested. I looked for "it" in academic accolades and boys. I was broken. I was hurt. My heart had a love deficit. I was a love child. My father loved me but didn't look at me lovingly. What he offered me constrained me. Even though he thought "it was love, it felt like hate.

I often wished he would have just talked to me, and I probably would have avoided seeking attention from them (the boys). They took me to the movies, played ball with me, and told me I was pretty and smart! It was for the wrong reasons; and for their personal motives. At the time I didn't know this, it felt like love, it looked like love, and I wanted it to be love. I needed a personal connection.

As my father's time with us under the same roof approached its end, my father's infidelity came to light and my mother was made aware. At the time my father was a minister, he preached. My father was heavily involved in church. Ironically, he had a relationship with the church that he didn't have with his family. I didn't understand why his connection to them was acceptable [what did "the church" have, that we didn't].

My father moved out, but my parents never divorced. We visited my dad on weekends and holidays, and he supported us financially. I believed he loved his family. I know he loved my mother. However, what I know about my father today and what I knew about my father then, caused me to see him differently.

I didn't know my father was a troubled man. He had the appearance of someone that had it all together, but he vehemently fought his own demons. When my father moved out of our home, he spiraled out of control. He developed a drinking habit and found himself in life-threatening situations. There was one incident that rendered a metal plate in his head and a crushed eye socket! My mother had a revelation from God regarding her role in my father's life. I recall her explaining to me, "I am assigned to your father to pray for him and believe God to deliver him from the hands of the enemy. I will remain faithful to my position"! I believed this revelation and my dad's personal challenges gave him insight into his life that nothing else could. It was God's power through prayer, fasting and unconditional love that transformed him into the man he was destined to become.

I realize, my father could not give what he did not possess. My father is a pivotal part of who I am and therefore I have embraced the positives, the negatives, and everything in between. Our identities are affirmed through the relationships we have with our fathers. It is clear to me, my challenged relationship with my dad developed daddy issues, but it does not mean he didn't want to be all I needed him to be. The healing and acceptance of my father was established when I understood he had matured from who he was... and was steadily evolving into who he would be.

Take Away Thought: *Brokenness is a part of the human experience. It does not disqualify you from becoming a parent, it does determine the quality in which you parent. Confronting the pain, hurt, and disappointment of your past; will empower you to embrace the power of your influence over your lineage.*

Chapter Two:

I AM LOIS' DAUGHTER

She is one of eighteen children, born to my grandmother. I cannot fathom what it feels like to be born into a family with seventeen siblings; constantly fighting to assert your identity and survive the seemingly unavoidable pain and hurt that is embedded in the dynamics of family.

My mother was raised in the Jordan Downs Projects in Watts, California, and this housing project has a notorious reputation. My family's lineage, it is one of the largest families in Watts.

My mother survived the era of racism and separation in the community that left physical and emotional scars. The Black Panther movement was in full effect, and my mother gloried in her recollections of the fight for equality. My mother appreciated "the finer things in life," thus, she protested to shop in stores that prohibited black patrons. Some time ago my mother told me about a shopping experience in Huntington Park; they [my mom and aunt] were brutally assaulted by the police. My mother was scarred physically and emotionally from this incident. I remember the fear I felt as I listened. Although, she exuded strength and courage as she told the story. Her upbringing was tough, and to know my mom was willing to die for what she believed in, stirs an unbreakable proudness within me.

My mother rarely spoke of her life before Christ because the Word of God told her, "Old things are passed away, and "Behold, you are a new creature in Christ," she believed this wholeheartedly! I can vividly tell you about my mom's post-Jesus days because as far as she was concerned her life before Christ was nonexistent. So, who was my mother? My mother was a prayer warrior. My mother was a believer. She was disciplined. My mother was a prophet.

My mother woke up before dawn and sought God early. She was a student of God's word and believed the proof was in the doing of His word. It boggled my mind as a child watching my mother study the bible because she was consumed by it. The Word of God intrigued her. She devoured of the word, and so sought to become it; living a Godly life guaranteed persecution and misunderstanding. "Jesus was misunderstood," was the mantra my mother lived daily! Consequently, she was unmoved by the perception and opinion of others.

My mother was the constancy of my life. My mother raised me in such a way that when I became a wife and mother, the task came naturally. Due to her diligence in God's Word, I was raised to live my life according to the Word; I am grateful for my upbringing but was often frustrated by it.

People recognized the anointing (God's presence) about my mom immediately. She had a dynamism that captivated onlookers. My mother was extremely comical, and she found humor in everything. Her favorite scripture was "This is the day that the Lord has made. I will rejoice and be glad in it [Psalms 118:24]." No matter how much turbulence she experienced in her life, she kept that scripture in her heart, and she blessed the Lord every day! It didn't matter whether the bills were paid, whether the food was on the table, whether my father did right or wrong, and when we [her children] were wayward; she had faith and believed no matter what the situation was–God would do what He promised. She was adamant about that.

My mother would not only tell me what to do, but she would explain the significance of why I should do it. When my mother ministered, she kept it simple. She said, "Jesus loves you…" and she believed in showing that love. She believed in being the church. As a child, my mother took my siblings and I to feed the homeless people that lived in our community. She didn't believe they should be hungry because we were there, and if we had food, then they had food. My mother's humility allowed her to talk with everyone. She shared the Gospel of Christ with anyone that listened [neighbors, addicts, prostitutes, or saints–no respect of person]. I grew up with love for people because she loved people. Her authentic relationship with God was beautiful. Expectantly, our lives did have its disadvantages, or so I felt! Quite frequently unrealistic expectations were imposed upon my siblings and I because we were "Lois' children."

My mother was the type of woman who always sided with what was right, no matter who it was! She often made a statement that I still laugh at today… She said, "Don't call me your mama when you're wrong." And I remember thinking, but not saying, "Then what should I call you, because I know I'm going to do something wrong." I was a mischievous child and often got in trouble because I was rebellious (plain and simple)!

Fortunately, the foundation my mother paved for me, always led me to God regardless of how good or bad my situation was! The first time I recognized that my mother had a gift I was in middle school, and I happened to skip class one day. My mother came to me and said, "God gave me a dream, and in this dream, you were ditching school…" I said, "Oh no, no, no, that was not me." And she said, "Oh it was you because God showed it to me." I silently asked, "God, why do you have to be a snitch?" What kind of God rats people out?

The night that my brother got shot, my mother had been in prayer for him. She went into her room and cried out to God for my brother and told us [me and my siblings] to get on our knees and pray too. Within an hour, my mother received a phone call stating my brother had got shot and rushed to the hospital. I understood at that moment that only God reveals the unknown, and he used my mother to do so.

I never felt good enough to be Lois' daughter. I often felt as if I was being watched; I felt restricted as always. Something constrained me from being my authentic self.

Early in life, I had identity issues because of who my parents were, my father, questioned his identity, and my mother walked boldly in who she was. I grew up feeling trapped, and I didn't know how to break free and simply be me.

I always felt honored to be her daughter. For a long time, I believed I was the only daughter. One day my brother said to me, "Do you know about Tina?" And I asked, "Who is Tina?" And he replied, "That was our sister." And I was like, "What do you mean that was our sister? Where is she?" He simply said, "She died." Immediately I had a complete understanding of why my mother was the way that she was towards me, why it seemed like we had an interpersonal relationship within our family... her first daughter died, and I never knew about her. Tina was not mentioned; often people refuse to talk about the most painful times in their life. My family was no different in that way.

I developed a new respect for my mother, a new understanding of her strength. It gave me insight as to why she loved Jesus so much. He healed the pain that no one else could! When my brother told me about Tina, I asked my mother about her. She said to me that God promised to give her another daughter, and He did. I was the manifestation of that promise, knowing this gave me a sense of purpose.

I felt empowered because at that moment I realized that I was destined to be here. The enemy tried to make me feel rejected... but God! I am Lois' daughter, God's promise... and knowing this means everything to me.

Take Away Thought: *Faith is the confidence you have in God. When your actions match what you say, your influence is multiplied. Our greatest influence impacts those closest to us, they are watching!*

Chapter Three:

INNOCENCE LOST

I never understood the unrelenting protection, love, and concern my family displayed until I was much older. As children, we do not [and cannot] fully delineate how impactful certain situations are. Fortunately, our parents are the covering that protects us from "what-could-be" or "should be." My parents, especially my mother did everything she could to keep me out of harm's way. Although her physical presence could not be physically ubiquitous, her prayers protected me even amid detriment.

I was only seven years old when I befriended him. He was not anyone's favorite; not even mine! I was attracted to the sadness in his eyes, all I wanted to do – is make him smile, but he lived in a broken place, and I was too naïve and young to take on such a burdensome task. I have always been a friendly person. I typically gravitate to people who seemed broken [my purpose in waiting].

"Jimmy" and I developed a budding friendship, and his gloominess seemed to be fading [slowly but surely]. One day while on the playground, Jimmy said, "Let's play over here!" it was secluded, but still within the authorized play area. Jimmy, kept trying to kiss me… but I said no! Jimmy didn't listen. Then he reached underneath my skirt and fondled me. I was speechless and petrified. This violator was my "friend," he was a child, and he was the first person to betray my trust.

I did not know how to properly respond or react to this violation! Consequently, I now understand my silence inadvertently permitted Jimmy to inflict the same hurt he experienced on to me. Although we were both children in this incident, we were both desecrated, and our innocence stripped away.

Jimmy violated me a second time, but this time he took his actions a bit further. His aggression escalated, and he was more forceful. He pushed me to the ground, laid his body weight on me, and humped on top of me. He didn't say anything; he seemed detached and dazed. He grinded his body on mine and virtually destroyed our friendship while he defiled my innocence. I knew Jimmy's actions were unacceptable. Ironically, I also knew Jimmy didn't understand what he was doing, but it was apparent that this had happened to him.

I never told anyone of these violations. I never spoke with Jimmy again. My distrust of men started here. My acceptance of abuse began here. My detachment from reality started here and more importantly, my silent scream echoed here.

Erratic behaviors and seemingly unexplainable decisions are always rooted in some form hurt. Anyone who is reading this, please understand when we fail to speak against wrongdoings [Parents teach your children to speak up and out] subconsciously we give the perpetrator permission to continue. We cannot allow unaddressed hurts to take root in our being. Emotional pain can be extremely detrimental to who we are. Please take note that I said "can be," because it can also be the very thing that propels us into the mandated purpose of our lives.

I am not excusing the violators of the innocent. However, I need my readers to understand that pain is inevitable… thus it can be used as a catalyst or an inhibitor. Fortunately,

God is the finisher of our faith and ultimately or fate. The pain can be and will be the catalyst for our greatness. God can make the very things that were meant to destroy us be the very things that construct the unavoidable path to our greatness.

Take Away Thoughts: *Our voice is one of the most valuable gifts given to us by God. We must not let the violations of others against us, silence us. Take back your power, use your voice, and allow your pain to propel you into your purpose.*

Chapter Four:

THE BURDEN OF BEING THE ONLY

I grew up as the only daughter in a family of five children. I have four brothers. I always felt the burden and the unsolicited expectations of being the only daughter. I was extremely loved, and my family rallied around me. However, the way that they loved me felt suffocating [to me], at the time. Apparently, everyone in my immediate family had the authority to tell me what I could and couldn't do… because I was the girl. Being a girl felt like a curse to me. I religiously heard, "You're a girl, so you shouldn't run outside." "You're a girl, so you shouldn't wear pants." "You're a girl, don't hang out with all those boys." "You're a girl, why are you playing basketball?" The monotony of this habitual "You're a girl" ideology, made me feel like "being a girl" was horrible!

However, being the only girl did have a few perks! My brothers and extended family catered to me. My brothers tried to protect me from everything… society, people, hurt and disappointment, and anything else they felt I couldn't or shouldn't handle! Nonetheless, I was inquisitive, and I possessed a natural curiosity about everything. I wanted to know how people lived, what's going on outside, I wanted to play, and I wanted to do all the things I was told I shouldn't do! Willingly, I rebelled. Either I was permitted to do what I wanted, or I chose to do it anyway.

Some people describe me as "the worst one." It is funny because I probably was. I was simply one of those kids! Although I was primarily well-behaved, it seemed as if the "bad" always overshadowed the "good."

By the time I reached in middle school, I had decided I was going to do what I wanted to do. I wore makeup and had my way of getting the boys' attention. I wanted them to see me. I wanted them to know I was in their midst. I wanted them to see how pretty I was and tell me! I began a pattern that would ultimately cost me more than I had bargained. I made wrong decisions, and I constantly battled who I was and who I pretended to be. Due to my parents' identity, I had to be one way in public and another way privately. But as far as I was concerned, I was merely "doing me!"

When I was in the 10th or 11th grade, my brothers found out I had a boyfriend. They made me feel like the "hoe of all hoes" because I was attracted to this guy. It was crazy! In our home, my natural attraction was apparently blasphemous! Armageddon had come because I liked a boy!!! The more they fought it; the more I chased it. The more that they told me I shouldn't, the more determined I became to do it. I refused to let them restrict my life. I was done with their "rules" at sixteen years old!

Everything I did at this point was contrary to what I was told to do by my family! I hung out, stayed with my boyfriend, I smoked marijuana. I even tried out for my high school football team and made it as the only female player! I fought the chains of restriction in my life. I was a wild child... I was named the prodigal daughter by my mother. I thought to myself... "Don't push me much harder, I haven't left yet, but I'm planning on it." I was just over it. I had never formed a relationship with Jesus Christ. I did what I had to do to keep my mom from riding me. I didn't want to get in trouble, so I went to church, prayed, and read the Bible; but God and I didn't have a "personal relationship."

Consequently, at 17 years old, I ran away. I remained gone for two weeks. It was the longest two weeks of my mother's life. I know she probably prayed harder than Jesus in the Garden of Gethsemane! Selfishly, I only considered my feeling, and I just had to get away! However, I was arrested for shoplifting because I had no money and they took me back home. My mother was frustrated and tired; her fight with me had diminished. Her physical ailments had gotten the best of her. When I was almost 18 years old, I left again.

This time I met a 34-year-old man, he was intriguing. He was well dressed, smelled of expensive cologne, and reminded me of my father. I didn't know it then, but this was the manifestation of my "daddy issues." You know what I mean, dating a man twice my age that reminded me of my father. We exchanged numbers and began hanging out. Before I knew it, I was impregnated by him on my 18th birthday. I hid my pregnancy because I just didn't know what to do. I tried to deny it. I pretended I wasn't pregnant. I imagined it would just go away, but my steadily protruding stomach proved the child inside me was real. I gave birth to my first-born son in secret and alone! Out of bewilderment and desperation I went home, I confessed my situation and begged my family to help me raise my son and they did!

I wasn't ready to be a mother. Again, I felt constrained, but I managed to remain present in his life for about a year. After that year, I confessed my apprehensions about motherhood, I told my mother, "I can't do it. You have to raise him. I'm not ready to be a mother. I'm just not ready…" and I stayed away!

Take Away Thought: *Live in the freedom of who you are, without the burdens, restrictions, or limitations of others. Refusing to quit will always require strength and courage, but it will also end in a more powerful you!*

Chapter Five:
WELCOME TO HOLLYWOOD

I left my mother's house, and I ran to the streets of Hollywood. Something about Hollywood drew me in. I was fascinated by its allure; the parties, the illusive-luxuriousness, and the possibilities. In Hollywood, I connected with people who were just like me. These were people who had run away from their homes, their problems, and their identity. Hollywood was a place of newness, acceptance, opportunities, and a place where I felt I was free "to just do me!" Hollywood was also a dangerous place to be, a place of misplaced identities, a place of hurt and pain, a place of the lost and confused.

I found myself on the streets of Hollywood, and I was quickly introduced to the drug life… from cocaine to methamphetamines, to pills and alcohol, and seemingly the most potent marijuana ever. My only inhibition was heroin because I heard it was nearly impossible to break your dependency but everything else was up for grabs! I partied every night, drank and smoked weed, and I did every drug available to get high. I was lost in a haze of deception camouflaged as freedom. Before I knew it, there were no remnants of the girl who grew up in a Christian home.

Cocaine was my drug of choice. It was easier to find. Everyone had it. It was at every party, and it looked "cool." It was just fun and games until I got addicted. My addiction was expensive and not just financially. I had come from a place where illegal drug distribution was the norm. I was familiar. I had seen it. I knew I could flip it and make it work for me... and I did just that!

I hung around people who were willing to put it in my hands. However, I didn't understand I became a slave to those people and to that drug. I became addicted crack cocaine. And my life spiraled out of control. I found myself in places I knew I didn't belong. I was in and out of jail on misdemeanors. I often pretended to be turning tricks, so I wouldn't face the harsh sentencing of drug charges.

I lived a life that should have created lifelong scars. Scars that only God could heal and make dissipate. I encountered men who wanted to take advantage of me, manipulate me, use me, and even try to pimp me. But, even in these places, I always knew God was with me.

He always manifested himself in a person, or a circumstance; especially during pivotal moments when I needed a way of escape. God promised in His Word, "I will never leave you, nor forsake you" [Hebrews 13:5]. I know this is true because there have been places and times in my life when I was in the slums! Fortunately, God manifested His presence and His power.

The first time I ever shot up I was at a party. I met an extremely attractive guy and he gave me all his attention. He constantly surrounded himself with beautiful women, but he claimed they were his friends. I wanted to get to know him, so we started hanging out. One day Mr. Fine introduced me to meth and I immediately felt my consciousness begin to leave; and the only thing I could think to do was SCREAM, "The Blood of Jesus, the Blood of Jesus, the Blood of Jesus..." and I came out of it! After that night, I never did another intravenous drug. I believe death knocked on my soul's door that night. I thought my last opportunity to get my life right with God had slipped away...but God spared me! His grace and His mercy saved me, but it wasn't enough. I went deeper into self-sabotage and destruction. I just chose never to do meth again.

Following this ordeal, I decided men would take care of me for anything and everything. On one night I met this guy that wanted to holler at me. He casually and conspicuously approached me and invited me to accompany him–I did. He opened the car door, placed me in the car and drove away from "the pretty city lights". I explained, "I don't know where we're going but as long as you know you're paying, I'm good!"

He became silent and his driving became careless. I felt afraid. We ended up in a secluded wooded area. He parked and turned off his lights. He came to my side of the car and snatched me out. He verbally degraded me and then he pummeled me unmercifully... I knew death was inevitable if he didn't stop. I cried and screamed but my screams seemed to fuel his violent attack. Then suddenly, his phone went off... my life was saved! He stopped beating me, looked at his red throbbing hand, and lugged me back inside the car. He nonchalantly dropped me off where we met, and unconcernedly drove away. I was physically relieved to be out of harm's way, but my mind needed an immediate escape!

I became a full-fledged "crackhead" and I lived in the underworld. It's the world that runs around beneath everything that's "right." It's the drug world, where people met in parking lots and passed illicit drugs. I slept all day and partied all night. My life was just getting worse and worse. Mr. Fine finally grew tired of me and decided he would pimp me out and beat me. He told me to "go out, "get "his" money and bring it back to him. I promised him I would. However, when I left I hopped on a bus and I never returned.

While on the bus, I hooked up with a young couple, they were headed to San Diego to make some money. We did everything I had done in Hollywood, but at a slower pace. I had hit my bottom, but not rock bottom; I was still trying to live "my life, my way." I continued to spiral out of control...

Take Away Thought: *There is no way to escape the ups and downs of life. Problems are inevitable and the attempt to assuage them with "recreational therapies" usually create bigger problems... but His grace is more than enough, and beyond what we deserve!*

Chapter Six:

I AM ADDICTED

*A*ddiction was my reality. I found myself in San Diego's underworld. Those who dwelled in the underworld, gravitate to each other. We found each other, and we fed off of one another! I learned how to use my gifts in a perverted way, nothing about my life glorified but God continued to extend His grace!

My drug addiction consumed my life, and I ended up homeless. I had nowhere to go. I found myself living nomadically in the streets of San Diego. I needed someone to help me... if not death would be unavoidable. I met a charismatic, "conscious" ex-con, he alluded me with his charm. He always told me that he saw something, but the very something he saw–he tried to suppress it. Our spiritual beliefs were opposites. Mr. Conscious believed in the ancestors, so he prayed to them. Although, I was not living for God I was convicted in my spirit.

I remember standing outside a church one day, I was hungry, and I had been in the same clothes for several days. My appearance deemed me to be homeless and addicted. Graciously, God led a Caucasian man to me in that instance. He came out of the church and approached me with loving concern. I knew this was a "But God" moment. He asked if I needed anything, offered to feed me, asked me where I was from, and who he should call. He said, "You don't belong here, and please know that God still loves you! Even in this state, you are still valuable to Him." This man showed me the love of God in its purest form. He was a stranger; he didn't know me, my mother, or my father! He knew nothing about me. He was simply on an assignment to tell me Jesus still wanted me.

That moment was a God intervention. In that moment God divinely intervened, and He was intentional about me! Jesus still loved me in my darkest hour, in my ugliest place, while I was at my worst. He still wanted me. Unfortunately, I was in a pit, my filthiness obscured my vision, and I questioned God's love for me! Instead of running to God in that moment, I attempted to run away... but I couldn't run from God; and Mr. Agape- Love walked me inside the church. He gave me food, tokens for the bus, a bag of toiletries, and other necessities. I was eternally thankful.

The relationship between Mr. Conscious and I continued... but it was established to help me! However, my impulsivity to run away kept me running, and Mr. Ex-Con came after me every time! He brought me into his home, cleaned me up, gave me food and money, and begged to just stay and get better! By the time he left for work, I was back out the door. Our connection reminded me of the story of Gomer going after his woman, which God told him to go after.

This tug-of-war between Mr. Conscious and I went on for several months. On a certain day I sauntered down the street, and I was high as a kite. Suddenly, I heard a voice say, "Go home, your mother is dying." I looked around questioning where the voice came from!?!? Then I heard it again, "Go home, your mother is dying." The only thing I could think to do was rebuke that voice because it had to belong to the devil and I said, "Satan, the Lord rebuke you." Dismissively, I continued to walk down the street and shortly after I was arrested.

I Am Addicted

Take Away Thought: *But God... is the explanation of the unexplainable. The situations that should logically have detrimental outcomes... but the exact opposite happens.*

Chapter Seven:

PRISON & PROMOTION

I knew when I got arrested this time I was "going away" for some time. My habitual offenses had worn the judge's patience and leniency. I was in Santee, California at Las Colinas Detention Facility. I called home because I knew prison was my fate. My mother answered the phone; her breathing was stressed and labored. Frantically, I asked her, "Are you okay?" She answered, "My nose is bleeding, and it won't stop, the ambulance is on way." Then she said, "I'm glad you're okay." I said, "I love you, mama." Without hesitation, she said, "I love you too."

I was still in a haze... I was not thinking clearly! Why didn't I connect "the voice" I heard with my mother's current state of being? The drugs had my head gone! I had been in jail nearly two weeks, and I decided to call home again to check on her. No one answered the phone. I returned to the sitting area of my confinement. A few minutes later the chaplain entered the pod area escorted by three correctional officers, he called my name. Immediately I asked, "What's going on?" The chaplain addressed me, "We have sad news." I asked, "What is it?" The Chaplin responded sorrowfully but quickly, "Your mother died."

The words "Your mother died" caused me to hyperventilate; in that moment my world changed forever. I stood there, crying and unaware. I realized I had not seen or spent any quality time with my mother in years! My addiction and need to run from my reality created unnecessary distance between my mom and I. The regret, the shame, the gut-wrenching pain swelled inside me like a hot-air balloon. I recall young lady that approached me soon after I got the news. She said, "I overheard you telling someone about your mother, and I want to pray with you." She opened the Bible to John 14, "Let not your heart is troubled. You believe in God, also believe in me. In my Father's house, there are many mansions. If it were not so, I would have told you. I go to prepare a place for you, and where I am there you will be also."

The harsh reality of my mother's death hit me like a tsunami. I went into a rage! The hurt, brokenness, and guilt consumed me [grief has no protocol]. My public defender got word that my mother had died. He informed me that he was working on a petition, so I could be released for my mother's funeral, I didn't know this process existed! I knew this was God manifesting His power, His strength, His love, His grace, and His mercy.

I went to court the next morning, and the judge released me for 14 days, which was unheard of! Now let me remind you, I'd been running since I was 17 ½ years old, and at the darkest moment of my life I had to attend my mother's funeral. Running, attempting to escape my reality was the only thing on my mind! I did not intend to turn myself back in. I called home and said, "Hey, I'm being released for mom's funeral and then I'm skipping states."

I went home and faced my family. I had not seen them in nearly two years! I returned to them a failure, a drug fiend, and a jail-bird. I could not endure the shame, guilt, and regret. Who would have my son now? My mother had been raising him. I was so afraid! I reverted to that 17-year-old who desperately needed her mother! I needed to see her. I could not believe she was gone.

I experienced a whirlwind of emotions as I walked into my mother's home. Knowing she was not there hurt me to my core. I felt suffocated, pained, and shattered. I saw the fights [between my parent and me, my mom and dad, and me and my brothers]! I saw it all in my head, it was almost too much to bear. I could see the moments at the dinner table. I looked to the kitchen and envisioned her standing there, but I knew she wasn't there. I couldn't dare walk into her room, so I slept in the living room. We lived in a small two-bedroom apartment for more than twenty years, my entire life existed in this place… and the only constant thing in my life was no longer constant. My momma was no longer available to me!

I regretted the years I wasted. I regretted the time I wished she was someone else. I regretted the times I didn't accept her for who she was. I had so much regret!!! I regretted the times I was so disrespectful. I regretted not loving my mother unconditionally! While sleeping in that house, something broke inside me that night…

We laid my mother to rest!! As I look at pictures of that day, my smile revealed a glimmer of hope. The joy I had during my mother's home-going service, was not attainable the night before. That day God gave me peace, strength, and power; I will never forget!

After my mother's funeral, I did as much as I could to help pack up her house, but I had to return to prison. At one point I was certain that I'd flee, thankfully I knew my life had to change. Something broke that night because I was ready to be accountable. I was ready to change my life. I said goodbye to my family [with finality]. My cousins Evelyn and Ross took custody of my son while I was in prison. Evelyn and Ross are nothing short of Servants from God!! They also took care of my mother in my absence.

During this time, my father had changed drastically. My father stepped up when my mom was diagnosed with cancer. He wasn't the man that raised me. He was different. This man was fun, talkative, and always concerned about my well-being. He assured me that he would take care of my son financially until I returned home.

I felt resolved when I turned myself back in. I had a great public defender, which was a manifestation of God's grace towards me again. He requested that I be placed in a mother infant program and I was approved. I was able to have my child there with me. At the time I had a second child on the way, yes, I was pregnant. The program was great; it allowed my father and my son to visit on the weekends. I saw a side of my father I had never seen. We talked and ate dinner together. Mr. "Don't Eat at the Table" was a changed man and it was awesome! He was an amazing grandfather. He was now comfortable in his identity. My father was confident, and it was evident he liked the man he was now. God restored our relationship.

I had two counselors I will never forget. Sharon and Faye, I am eternally grateful for them. They saw something in me and demanded me to release it, and my life changed because of it. I received counseling and rehabilitation through behavior modification. Therefore, when I was released I had two options: I could either assimilate back to a community or go into an extended aftercare program with my children. I knew I wasn't strong enough [yet] to have so much independence. I couldn't take a chance… the odds were against me. I witnessed so many women return to prison, like a revolving door. I knew I could not take that chance; I needed a "lasting" change!

My kids and I went into the aftercare rehabilitation program for parolees at Providence Place. It was a phenomenal place of transition; I realized the change had to become a lifestyle. I developed lasting relationships and I learned how to have fun without drug usage. Providence Place changed my life. Eventually, I was offered a job through the program and started working at a car dealership. I began the process of rebuilding my life, it wasn't easy, but it was worth it! I made conscious deliberate efforts to change! I refused to relapse, it was common and at times it felt inevitable. There was one principle I knew was true, I had seen the evidence of growth and change. It was simple... Do your work! It meant you had to work on yourself, self-analysis, self-reflection, and self-confrontation.

Take Away Thought: *Life has a way of teaching us our greatest lessons through our greatest pain. We must challenge ourselves and the systems in which we live to have a significant change in our lives.*

Chapter Eight:

LAID TO REST

After I was released from rehab, I wanted to salvage the relationship between my daughter's father and me. Our daughter was born while I was in the Mother Infant program. To my surprise, my daughter's father was now abusing drugs. He was a disciplined man and a member of a major black prison affiliation. He stood against the very thing that had now consumed him! When I saw him that way it broke my heart, but I felt I owed him my loyalty. I vowed to help him in the same way he had helped me… so I stayed with him. I stayed with him even though part of me was dying inside. My new identity cringed at what used to be me… and we conflicted constantly. My daughter's father and I always had issues with each other. Fortunately, my relationship with my dad helped me through this tumultuous phase.

My father was such a changed man! His loving and kind demeanor helped form an amazing friendship between us. He called me every morning, I didn't call him. He was cheerful and sincerely concerned about me and his grandchildren. I finally had the type of father-daughter relationship I had always desired... and he helped me sort through my relational issues by simply showing me what I needed in a man – through my newly established relationship with him.

On July 25th, just two days before my birthday my dad called me before work. This had become our routine. We discussed the possibilities of my birthday festivities. Later that day, my brother called me. He asked, "Are you sitting down? I replied, "No, no I'm not sitting down." He said, "Well you should." So, I sat down, and my brother said, "Daddy died today." The room spun, I shook my head in disbelief, I didn't understand this turn of events... I didn't want to understand! My father was a healthy man. He worked every day. He ministered, and he had become one of my closest friends! I loved him and now Daddy was dead.

Thankfully, my father and I had solidified a strong relationship that was enriched by our monthly visitation routine (even after I had been released from prison). Nobody knew I was in town. I didn't tell anyone I was coming, just daddy. I went to his house, with the kids and spent the weekend with him. This routine had been established for months; it was wonderfully beautiful! It was God's grace and mercy that allowed my father and I to have the relationship that we had prior to his death; I am eternally grateful to God for it! I finally knew my daddy loved me, cared about me, he encouraged me, believed in me, and most importantly he desired a closer relationship with me.

Shortly after my father's death, my nephew was murdered. I grew up with my nephew, I felt like my world was coming to end! I didn't want to go back to what I knew; I couldn't relapse–not now! Something had to break. Something had to happen. What do I do? I decided to go home, and I fought the urge to assuage my pain with the numbness I knew drugs delivered. I prayed to God, "Please don't let me go back!" Then it got worse...

On February 4th, my daughter's father and I got into an explosive argument because I refused to give him our rent money for drugs! Things went from bad to worse quickly, the verbal altercation became physical! Mr. Conscious put his hands on me and I said, "Oh, hell no!" I had received enough love from and fatherly wisdom from my dad to know I did not deserve that. I deserved to be loved, adored, respected, honored, cherished, and to simply be treated like a lady! BD wasn't giving me that, so I called the police and they arrested him. The officers asked if I wanted to press charges. I said, "No, I'm not." They warned me that he would be released in 24 hours. I said, "I'll be long gone by then!"

On February 5th, my life turned for the better! I used my rent money to buy a Datsun 500. Ironically, it was the same kind of car my dad had when I was a kid, but it was orange. Something about that fact gave me power and strength. So, I bought it and did not know how to drive it! Go figure! It was a stick–my dad always drove a stick. I was like whatever, I didn't care. At this point in my life, nothing was going to keep from moving forward. I vowed to learn how to drive a stick that day! Same attitude just now my focus was different. The car owner taught me how to drive it in 30 minutes. He said listen now you know how to get to fifth gear. When you get on the freeway shift to fifth gear and ride it all the way to L.A. Don't stop until you get there! That's exactly what I did. I packed all the clothes that I could fit in the back of the Datsun. I left everything that resembled anything of what I had or used to be. I left it there. I left it to burn in the ashes of my past. I pressed forward and changed courses; I drove home. My family wasn't ready for me or expecting me. My two-hour drive felt like six. I had so many questions, so many thoughts! What could I say? What would they say? It didn't matter. I was going home. Although my thoughts and uncertainty plagued me, I kept going. I was different; I had changed for the better. My family didn't know, but they were going to find out.

My cousin Lisa insisted, "Girl come stay with me." I moved into her apartment, my kids and I slept on her the floor of her one-bedroom apartment. I was grateful, and my life started over. I felt like I could finally breathe...

Take Away Thought: *Starting over at times means going back to face that thing(s) you have been running from. Fear of the unknown is your imagination misinformed, take control of those thoughts and overcome it by confronting it.*

Chapter Nine:

SINGLE & A MOTHER

    *E*veryone was excited to have me back. However, I saw the doubt in their eyes, the wonder! "Is she really clean?" "Has she changed?" "Is this real or will she leave again? Without hesitation, I worked overtime to show them I was different. Assuredly, they soon realized my change was real. I developed higher standards for myself.

    I had been exposed to people who were overachievers. I had lived in Hollywood with celebrities and people who earned millions of dollars, they owned their homes, and were business-savvy regardless of their habits! My exposure to these things gave me a different outlook. Retrospectively, I was ahead coming from behind. My mindset extended beyond mediocrity, even as an addict. I possessed a Go-getter's mentality!

I had decided that romantic-relationships would be on the back-burner for a while! Honestly, I didn't care if I ever got into another relationship because I was wounded, battered, and scarred. I knew I needed to heal. I needed to be whole. I needed Jesus!

When we come to Jesus we are a mess. We are dirty, just filthy, and He cleans us up. But even in the cleansing, God still desires a complete surrender from us! I had reached a place of surrender... and I was ready to surrender but I didn't know how. What did it mean to surrender? I had access to catchy slogans and numerous scriptures that spoke of surrendering to God... But I needed practicality. I needed someone or something to make it plain!

The remnants of my past still affected me. My knowledge of hustling did not dissipate, and in all honesty, I still hustled. I no longer used any drugs but, I sold weed. I was Ms. Mary Jane, Ms. Burning 50, Ms. Loud because I knew how to hustle. I worked during the day and I hustled at night. I had just started over, I needed a car, my own crib, and I was a single mother... Somebody do the math.

What was I going to do? This is the first time I really had to fend for myself. I didn't have supplemental income. I didn't have a man taking care of me. It was just me and my two kids. I was single, and I was a mother. Please take notice of the separation of the two words... far too often people treat the terms single and mother as one phrase... and technically and realistically it is not! Singleness and motherhood are quite complicated because it's natural to desire a relationship but brokenness and hurt have your heart and mind jacked all the way up! However, because the obligation of being a mother takes precedence over emotional imbalance, Momma must suck it up in order effectively care for her children and nurture them.

Consequently, I fought the need to hustle and my need to give everything to God. Unfortunately, I didn't know how to trust God and I didn't know what it looked like. Momentarily, in my proudness... I almost convinced myself that "Trusting in God" looked like me not going to jail for selling weed to support my kids... I knew that was a deceptive rationality straight from the devil! Then it dawned on me, "Faith and trust in God" looked like my mother!

I had flashbacks of my mother depending on God to do something in our home. She didn't go out and hustle. She knew how to hustle but she didn't! I was convicted, and I knew prayer was the answer to my apparent conflict of interest. Slowly, I drew closer to God through prayer. God caused me to remember conversations I had with my mother, I hadn't recalled in years... and special moments with my father that was still freshly marinated.

My father's words came to me, and I contemplated going back to school, but I didn't have the confidence. Truth be told, I didn't do so wonderfully in school because I was lazy, and I thought being cute was enough! I finally got into my own place, just me and my two kids. It felt good to have my own. After talking to God, I considered the elimination of my hustle; but the money was good! What did I want more, God or money?

My new neighbor and I hit it off immediately! She was mad cool and funny. Many days we sat and talked about life, our pasts, and our children. She often watched the kids for me when I had to work, and I kept a little extra change in her hands. I still had my side hustle, the money kept calling me! I was ready to date again. It had been almost a year and my neighbor encouraged it, even watched my kids if I met a worthy suitor. Anyway, Ms. Neighbor always talked about her son. He was incarcerated, and he had recently professed to her in his letters that he had given his life to God. He seemed excited about his newly attained liberation. I was empathetic and open minded to my neighbor's happiness regarding her son, because I had been there! However, I didn't know it at the time, that I was becoming emotionally connected to a man I had never met.

For some reason, June 12, 2012, was significant. The night before, Ms. Neighbor asked me to pick her son up from the bus station and I agreed. I really didn't want to, but she looked out for me regularly, so I felt obligated to do this small favor. I got up early to pick him up from the bus station before I went to work. When I got there, he wasn't anywhere in sight... I became quite perturbed. I decided it was no big deal and I went to work.

When I arrived home from work that day, Ms. Neighbor ran over to my house and happily exclaimed that her son had made it home. I was happy for her, but I was still slightly irritated because her son's absence at the bus station had thrown my day off. I begin to prepare dinner for my kids immediately because I' still hustled. People were calling because they needed their "high."

Unexpectedly, there was a knock on my door; it was Ms. Neighbor's son. I opened the door... and I must be honest and just keep it real, this man was younger and more attractive than I imagined, there was something about this dude that kind of struck me from the moment I saw him! I tried to contain myself and keep my composure. However, maintaining a straight face was so hard! He had that fresh out of prison physique, a bright white smile, and the manners of gentlemen. I was excited on the inside and calm, cool, and collected on the outside.

Take Away Thought: *I hope when real love shows up, you are wise enough to recognize it, you are healed enough to receive it, and possess enough fight to keep it!*

Chapter Ten:

THE BEST: SAMUEL GILMORE

*Q*uite often, some of the best things in our lives, come by accident, or so we think. They come when we least expect them in the most unexpected ways. These things often take our lives from good to better, and better to best! These gifts always contain what's best for us and change our lives forever... Allow me to introduce "The Best," my hubby, my bae, my forever – Samuel Gilmore!

I met this guy named Samuel on June 12th, 2006; most people called him Texas. He had just been released from prison and I was in a transitional state... trying to go from good to better. I'd been selling weed for a long time and it was just time for it to come to an end. Fatefully, in my life any time I needed to start or end a chapter, it always involved a man. Sometimes it was good, and sometimes it was bad. But this time–it was the best.

Sam and I were kind of feeling ourselves. There was a tangible energy between us. I had spent a lot of time healing from my past, writing, and talking to God about the things I had experienced in my previous relationships... and I knew I was ready to move forward. I briefly talked to a few dudes, but nothing was serious, just a few numbers that I called when boredom struck.

In the meantime, I had the opportunity to get to know Samuel. We became friends and developed an authentic intimacy. He intrigued me because he had an old soul... although he was a young guy. We talked about everything; our lives, prison, slanging, and our relational experiences. He was very uncomfortable knowing I sold weed, and his discomfort made me uncomfortable.

I came to cherish our friendship. I enjoyed his company and I looked forward to coming home because I now had another reason to knock on Ms. Neighbor's door. However, Samuel wasn't pushy; I spent time with my kids, and did my motherly duties. Then Sam and I would chill, we formed a bond that was simplistic yet secure. We sat outside on the stoop and talked for hour and hours. The things I shared with him, I had never shared with anybody else... it was weird because I had just met this dude! But there was something about him that allowed me to be transparent.

I freely expressed myself, it was the most authentic that I had ever been in my entire life! He made me feel so comfortable. I had such a "potty-mouth." I often told people I'd curse them out creatively, because I looked at it as an art form because I loved words. I had always loved words, profane or not. On one occasion "I went-off" on somebody and he looked at me and said, "I don't like women that curse." He said, "That is not cool." It became a priority to stop cursing and it wasn't as hard as I thought because he made me want to be better.

I had never encountered a man that made me want to obey him; that made me want to submit to him, I found myself doing whatever he liked! The attraction was irresistible! However, he had his own personal issues. His status made it extremely difficult for him to get a job, so he couldn't find work. Sam's mother had to move, and her new place could not accommodate him.

One day he walked up to me and said, "Hey, I don't know what I'm going to do." I replied, "Well what's going on?" He said, "You know, my mom is moving, and I don't have nowhere to go out here. And I don't know what I'm going to do. I think I'm going to go back to Texas." And I responded, "Well if you go back to Texas, what are you going to do there?" He was like, "The only thing I know how to do – hustle." The same man that had talked me out of hustling was now in the situation where he felt his only option was to hustle.

I knew he didn't want to do it, but our conversation soon went silent. The uncertainty made talking uneasily. I didn't know what to do. Instinctively, I remembered my father telling me that he became a forklift operator after he left the military. Then I recalled an advertisement for forklift operators in a local warehouse that employed felons.

The next day Sam and I conversed. I said, "There's this place if you pay them $60 and they'll give you a forklift license, and you can go get a job at an agency with that forklift license for a warehouse, they hire felons." And he said, "I don't have enough money to do that." And I gave him $60 because I was feeling him and I believed in him.

I did not want Sam to leave. I had not felt that way about anyone in a while; it had been 1yr and 4 months to be exact. That was my primary reason for helping him. Secondly, I felt like he needed a break. He was a black man who needed the help of a black woman to get on his feet and whether I was his girl or not, I had a responsibility to him as a sister to help him. I think it was humanity, the seeds of humanity that my mother planted within me. I gave him the money without expectation. I gave it to him because I wanted him to have a fighting chance. I wanted him to have an opportunity to get his life together.

The very next day, when I got home from work, Sam knocked on my door and showed his forklift license. The smile on his face, the pride in his stance, and the hope in his eyes revealed the gradual redemption of his manliness. Within a few days, he had a job, and he was going to work. But we had another dilemma. He didn't have anywhere to go. So, I had to decide. I'm not saying it was the right decision, but it was the decision that I made at that time. I must be transparent, I moved him on my couch.

It was so difficult, and I was torn because I had two kids and I felt I was not being the person I should be for them. Then again, there was something about this man that I couldn't allow to walk out of my life. I just couldn't let him get away. There was something brewing in my spirit that this relationship was not comparable to any of my previous relationships. There was a peace in my spirit that assured me he was different.

The experiences that we shared made me realize he was someone I had to keep close to me! It was during the Christmas holidays; my daughter was sick with pneumonia at the time. Samuel was neither my daughter's father nor my husband. However, he offered his support and presence every time I went to the hospital. He genuinely cared! His concern left me speechless, and he solidified how "different" he was in that moment!

Shortly after this, he moved from my couch to my bedroom. I knew my "shacking-up" was not a good look, but it was my truth and decision. Over time, Samuel formed authentic relationships with my children. When I prepared meals, he played football with my son or helped them with their homework. If I needed something fixed around the house or I needed my car washed – he did it. I never asked or coerced him into doing anything for me or the kids! I don't know if his actions were strategic, but they worked!

Our connection was unlike anything I had felt before. When he officially asked if I would be his girlfriend, I was ecstatic! One day he casually said, "Hey, would you be my girlfriend?" I was like, "Yeah! I will be your girlfriend, your bae, your boo – all of that!" We grew leaps and bounds as a couple; it was us against the world because no one really supported the relationship.

My family thought Sam was my "boy-toy" because of our age difference. Other onlookers believed I needed a baby-daddy replacement, but we didn't allow anyone to define the depth of our relationship. They were looking from the outside in and we [Sam & I] accepted each other from the inside out. Consequently, the formulation of "Team Gilmore" was inevitable, we fought for our status, our truth, and most importantly our commitment to each other. Our love was pure, thus we remained rooted in each other–because love established our foundation and we both had made the sacrifices.

Samuel's vision for our life as a couple has always been admirable and inspirational! When we were dating, we often hung-out with other couples... Sam would say things like, "I'm going to buy us a helicopter." And I would be like, "Oh, Jesus. You can't say stuff like that, Bae you have to stop it!" People will think we are crazy." Nevertheless, my reprimands did not compel him to stop declaring greatness for us, no matter what it was. This man talked about buying acres of land and building our homes (note that homes are plural) and I became frustrated because I had no vision.

The people I grew up around barely owned furniture and Sam spoke of owning the land that contained the homes that housed the furniture! I mean, I grew up in a two-bedroom apartment my entire life… owning acres of land was not a part of my plan! How was I supposed to wrap my mind around this; I didn't have vision! Then along comes Samuel into my life and he is a visionary! I didn't understand how important it was to have a man that had the vision, so I fought his vision, every chance that I got because I didn't know any better.

Slowly but surely, I adopted his visionary mentality. The more I loved and embraced his vision as our vision, our love grew deeper. The more I cared about him, the more I listened to what he had to say, and before I knew it, he had infiltrated my heart and my world… and it felt like heaven on earth! Together we developed a mindset that we were in this [our relationship] to keep this. We decided whatever God wanted to do in our life as a couple we were open to it! God drew us even closer together.

Samuel asked me to stop selling weed and I did. What bae wanted from me, bae got it – every time! There was something about Samuel Gilmore that made me want to do right. I wanted to submit to him. It was almost unthinkable;

because I was adamantly certain I would never submit to any man. My mother had submitted to my father and look how that turned out. I didn't know then the strength and power it took to submit; to be viewed as weak to preserve the other's strength. However, I found out quickly just how powerful submission is, even when it hurts.

Sam and I both understood God had brought us together, and God's plan for our life included holy matrimony. Sam and I met in June of 2006... Sam popped the question in February of 2007... and I said "Yes," immediately!

Take Away Thought: *True love is the manifestation of God in our lives. When love manifests itself authentically–it is unmistakable... and it will be patient, kind, long-suffering, enduring, sacrificial, and it will produce the promise of greatness [the best]!*

Chapter Eleven:

THE PROMISE

After we solidified our engagement, we came to the conclusion that we must honor God! We vowed to commit to celibacy until we were Mr. &. Mrs. Samuel Gilmore. We spent a year planning our wedding; we were excited and eager to say, "I Do". As we grew in every way, our relationship with God became our focus. We struggled with our routine, we lived together and that was not in alignment. It wasn't what we believed God wanted for us. We couldn't afford to live in separate apartments and pay for our wedding. It was time for us to become more disciplined; we decided we were going to stop having sex. Our convictions were getting the best of us, but our bodies were calling for each other. This seemed impossible, but it became our motivation to get the wedding completed.

We were excited about new opportunities, change, and growth! Sam and I desired more; more of God, more of His guidance, and more of His Will to continually manifest in our lives. Fortunately, we understood obedience is the prerequisite for God's provision. Consequently, shortly after we married, we obeyed God and relocated to Lake Elsinore, California. God gave us favor with a couple who owned a townhome, and we moved-in. They were Christians from New Zealand; and they told us, God gave them a peace about us as their tenants; we were given the keys that day!

Sam and I were ready to have a baby. I was elated to become impregnated by my husband, and not my boyfriend. Sam didn't have any children; thus, he was simply ready to be fruitful and multiply. Initially, we were simply enjoying being newlyweds; and experiencing guilt-free sex! There's something about guilt-free sex that is just heavenly. However, after a year of trying, we still hadn't gotten pregnant. Naturally, we were concerned, so I scheduled an appointment with my physician. I had recently stopped taking birth control, and the doctor informed us this was "normal…" and said, "Take your time!"

Another year that went by and we still had no baby. Our concern turned to fear. Fortunately, God gave us to have marriage mentors, my aunt, and uncle. They have 43 years of marriage, wisdom, knowledge, understanding, and simplistic marital applications under their belts; but Sam and I were just getting started and we had hit a hard spot… They prayed with us, believed with us, and told us to trust God's timing.

It was so hard finding work here in this new place. Sam and I were both on unemployment for approximately two years. At that time, 33% of the country was unemployed. I now know the delay of our child was God allowing us to grow together, but we wanted our baby, now. Yet another year had passed, and our multiplying still hadn't started. We were on the brink of hopelessness and devastation.

I desperately wanted to give my husband a baby; and every time my menstrual cycle came, I cried. I felt like a failure! Why was able to have children by men who didn't want them; and unable to give a child to the one man in my life who desired nothing more than fatherhood! I felt like God was punishing me. I didn't believe any other explanation was plausible?

Six years into our marriage we received our miracle. I know what I am about to release sounds crazy, but it is our absolute truth. One afternoon, my husband and I were making love, our bedroom window was open. Suddenly, we felt a rushing wind come through the window. This wind was not a flowing breeze; it came in thrusting – but it wasn't windy outside! This wind is so powerful that we stopped, looked at each other cautiously, and simultaneously said, "What was that?" It was an unexplainable wind. I know now, it was the Wind of God that engulfed our bedroom and bodies that day.

Our intimacy grew deeper in that moment of the unexplainable wind! We acknowledged it and loved every minute of it. Afterwards, we laughed about it; but we both knew – something happened! We kept saying something happened. It was like a huge inside-joke between him and I. We never told anyone [until now]! Anyway, who would believe us? We barely believed it ourselves… it just didn't make sense!

Approximately a few weeks later, my daughter complained of chest pains and shortness of breath. I rushed to the emergency room. I told my husband to stay home with our son, and that I'd call when I got there.

Once we arrived, I heard God say, sign-in for both of you and tell the doctors you need to take a pregnancy test. I simply told God "I am not pregnant," repeatedly and with an attitude! My unbelief was as bad as Peter's denial of Jesus as his homeboy! However, Daddy- God was relentless with that voice. I just could not ignore it, no matter how hard I tried! Begrudgingly, I signed up for the pregnancy test, I did it just to prove HIM wrong!

They asked me for a urine sample, and my daughter had been miraculously healed of her chest pains. She looked at me nonchalantly, and said, "Mommy, I'm fine we can go home now." I replied, "Honey, we didn't come all the way here for nothing. The doctors have to verify that you're okay." The nurse returned and asked me to come outside. I stepped outside the room, and she said, "There's something I need to tell you." I said, "Okay." She quietly squealed, "You're pregnant." I heard her, but it did not register. So, I asked her again, "What did you say?" She said, "You're pregnant, "I'm not supposed to tell you this, but I felt like you needed to know. I'm supposed to let the doctor tell you, but I felt you needed to know right now."

I stood there in shocked disbelief! I began to cry. I said, "I hear what you're saying, but let's play a little game..." and I said, "Blink once for yes and twice for no." She blinked one time. Again, I said, "Wait a minute. Maybe you didn't hear me. I said blink once for yes and blink twice for no." Comprehensively, she blinked one time again, and I COLLAPSED–on the inside. I collapsed inside because this was the day that the Lord had promised. I REJOICED because of the promise. The child God promised me, just like He had promised my mother regarding me! Infertility was defeated that day!

I didn't know how or what I'd say to Sam... so I just called. He immediately asked, "How is she, how is everything going? I blurted out, "I have something to tell you." Sam said, "What babe?" I replied, "I'm pregnant." He said, "How do you know that?" I said, "Well, I took a test, and they said I'm pregnant." And, he said, "Oh, all right". "Can you bring me some tacos back from Jack in the Box?" I think his shock responded more than happiness in that moment!

We had a rocky pregnancy. My husband had recently gotten a job as a truck driver, and he was constantly away from home. I had not imagined our first pregnancy as a couple to be like this! He was on the road 25 days a month, and home the other five days. At the very same time, our home life was experiencing some turbulence! We were challenged in every way. The enemy fought the very promise that God gave us from every angle!

I received a phone call from my doctor's office during my second trimester. The young nurse said, "Your Down syndrome test came back, and your baby will be born with Down syndrome." I didn't know how to process what she said… I couldn't understand! Why would God make us wait so long for a baby, and then add health complications to His promise? I didn't understand that I couldn't understand that, and I refused to accept that!

Thankfully, we found out that our daughter did not have Down syndrome. It wasn't true. This was an attack of the enemy that tried to diminish our faith, disturb our peace, disrupt our home, and cause tension between Sam and I... and it almost did! We were both preoccupied with how we felt individually and not as a marital unit! Sam NEEDED me, and I didn't cover him in prayer… I was too engrossed in my own self-pity and our home issues. Moreover, I needed him, but he was on the road working to PROVIDE for us. What should have been a time of bliss and preparation became a time of unexpected tribulation.

Take Away Thought: *God does not schedule our blessing on our time clock, they are pre-destined and are granted to us by His grace! It is for us to believe by faith, that He will perform every promise He makes!*

Chapter Twelve:
PROMISE PROBLEMS

I learned through experience whenever God speaks promise over our lives, it will be accompanied by problems. The promise of our marriage proclaims, "Till death do us part!" However, when I was 8.5 months pregnant, an emotional death tried to creep into our marriage…I was about four weeks away from delivery, and I was blindsided by a blast from my husband's past.

My husband was constantly on the road due to his trucking profession. However, he desperately wanted to be home with me, so he could support our family. The distance and strained-communication between us caused frustration and sadness. Samuel was depressed because his manly obligation to work and support his family kept him from experiencing the beautiful journey of pregnancy. Meanwhile, I simply tried to survive pregnancy without my husband's presence.

Without fail, a foreseeable problem crept into our marriage. While Sam was on the road, social media became his refuge. He connected with a female-friend, they chatted frequently. They started to have conversations because she was available to speak to him when I wasn't. During those long drives at night, she was available to take his call. She didn't present herself as a "promise-problem," so he talked to her about the promise! The feeling between my husband and his "friend" started to grow... and emotional infidelity tried to steal the breath of life from our marriage.

I'll never forget the night I confronted my husband about her. He was asleep, and his phone was at the edge of the bed... I have kept it real up until this point and I won't stop now. Honestly, I had NEVER been that chick. Samuel didn't even have a code on his phone because I simply didn't get down like that. I had a self-assured confidence and if my man didn't recognize that, then shame on him. So, snooping through his phone was the equivalent of lowering my standards... and I wasn't about to do that or was I?

Unexpectedly, I heard that voice; ladies [and gentlemen] you know that voice! That voice of intuition, that voice of instinct, the voice of GOD-himself! It was that voice... the voice that continually guided me through so many situations in my life. The voice I valued and had learned to never ignore again. I knew it was God. I just didn't understand why God told me to look through his phone. I simply didn't think God would tell me to do something I considered a sure sign of "insecurity!"

Therefore, I sat in the chair [next to our bed] and contemplated for nearly two hours. I literally argued with God... I whispered angrily [whispering while you are mad as HELL makes you look crazy as HELL]. Anyway, through gritted teeth I said "God, why are you telling me to do this!!! I am not looking God... NO, no, no! I refused to do it, I crossed my arms, poked out my lips, and warm tears rolled down my cheeks because I didn't want to face the reality of what I was about to see...but I listened to God!

I scrolled through his phone; I was not only in shock, I was in utter disbelief. Immediately, my anger arose, and I demanded Sam wake up. He wasn't babe or honey, He was Sam... [I thoughtfully thanked God because the old me would have at least had some hot grease or a 44-bulldog revolver].

My anger was exceeded being mad; I had leveled up to cray-cray! I yelled and screamed, "Who in the hell is this, and how long have you two been planning to hook up? I just knew that was the plan because all the messages insinuated it for the most part. There were a few texts about our household issue problems and that angered me even more! He was telling this chick all our business and I could not make myself react calmly.

Samuel stood there and accepted the fault for his actions completely... and I took off! I started pummeling him with full force, and he just stood there – and took every forceful blow and never raised his hands from his side. My husband was totally contrite and accepted what he felt he deserved. I stopped suddenly and wept uncontrollably because I willfully inflicted pain on the man I loved. Some of you reading this might say he deserved it, I beg to differ. I was out of control and completely out of pocket! No one deserves to be hit!

It was one o'clock in the morning, and I called her from his phone. Of course, she answered because she believed it was Samuel, but to her surprise it was me. I asked her had she slept with my husband and she assured me they had never slept together. Then she admitted she was wrong but attempted to justify her actions with the excuse of loneliness and the confession that they were "just friends."

I was done listening; I berated her with introspective questions. I didn't want her answers. I just wanted her to think about what I was saying and how I felt! So, I asked, "Why would you allow any married man to put you in this situation?" "Don't you know he is never going to leave me and has never planned on leaving me?" I asked her, "Why would you betray another woman by plotting to sleep with her husband while she's 8.5 months pregnant, with his baby?!?" I asked her, "Why don't you do yourself a favor and love yourself more than this, respect yourself more than this, and more importantly PROTECT yourself more than this!" I turned to him with the phone on speaker, I asked him, "Were you planning on leaving me?" He replied, "No." I asked, did he want to be with her, he replied No again! Lastly, I said tell her, DON'T EVER CALL AGAIN! There was nothing more to say, to either of them! I hung up the phone

This was the longest night of my married life and daylight crept into our home at the rate of molasses. We contacted our marriage mentors that next day and explained what happened. We told them everything and the next day

Sam went back out on the road for work. I was broken and betrayed, and I didn't see how I could move forward!

My husband was supposed to be different, not like the other men in my life. While I was in prayer the next day, God said "Forgive him", I said "What!" really God! Forgive him, I don't know how!" But God wanted me to forgive him, and I obeyed. I called Sam, and when I heard his voice–I broke down. I said I'm not giving up on you. I refuse to give up on us, I love you! I forgive you!! He broke down at this point and said I thought I had lost my family. I didn't know what you were going to do... I allowed Sam to finish confessing his truth to me, and then I hung up the phone softly.

My weariness said, "Okay God, what now?" Sam and I tried to heal and rebuild our trust, our love, and our marriage for several weeks. We talked about everything, the why, the when, the how, and the what. He felt lonely because of the problems in our home, not to mention I was sick and pregnant. His job caused him to miss our first pregnancy [together], an experience we waited more than six years to have. Our life was in turmoil, but I understood how this happened [Infidelity is one of the most probable causes of marital dysfunction, in 33% of all marriages one or both partners admit to cheating; and this number increases to

43% during pregnancy]. We needed to put this behind us and move forward.

My scheduled C-section had finally arrived. We checked into the hospital and our beautiful healthy promise-child was born with the song "Happy" by Pharrell playing in the background. Unfortunately, another promise-problem surfaced. There is always something lurking... I had my surgery at 8:00 am and I was transported to the maternity ward by 11:00 am. However, I was in excruciating pain, but I was determined to get up and move around. At 2:30 pm, I went for a walk. When I returned Sam and I took a nap. I woke up before him; our baby was in the nursery. Then I heard that all too familiar voice again, says "Look in his phone..." I shook my head feverishly in disagreement. My heart dropped, and sadness consumed me.

I looked in the phone, and my husband had sent her pictures of my newborn baby!! Jesusssss! TAKE THE WHEEL, because I am about to set him on fire!! I couldn't believe this man [my man] was still in contact with this chick! The broad still answered his calls! I decided at that moment, she could have MY husband!

Of course, I woke him up, but only to dismiss him from my room and ultimately my life. I was good, I deserved better and

I did nothing to deserve the continued betrayal. I was sure of it; at this point, I was in too much pain and grief to deal with it. I was angry, belligerent, and I felt like I couldn't tell anyone because I wanted to protect him. While I was dying inside, questioning myself, and everything about my marriage. We were taught to keep our problems in our marriage! Despite what happened, I didn't want to rob him of this precious time, even though I felt they had robbed me blindly. I love my husband infinitely, and even amid unspeakable hurt... death is the only thing that will separate me from him.

Truth is, there was an emotional connection they had formed. I could not understand what she was giving him that I wasn't. I had to ask and demanded the uncut truth. He said it was easy to talk to her, she listened without interrupting, and they don't talk about "problems." He said, "Sharon all we do is talk about problems!" I knew He was right, it was the truth. It was all true and I was forced to take accountability for not creating the atmosphere of open communication. I had to take responsibility for my shortcomings, it wasn't his entire fault. That didn't justify his actions, but it explained the separation between us that the enemy used to try and destroy our unity.

I made a commitment to allow him to speak freely, I needed to hear his heart–no matter how I felt! He had to ask God to cut the emotional ties; and he severed all social media connections, changed his number, and deleted hers. We had to start fresh; it was up to us to change the course our marriage. We were both responsible for the state of our marital union. It was difficult at times because it was easier to remember rather forget. We had to be intentional about the healing and forgiveness process!

It was not easy, but we knew it would be a part of our testimony. We prayed together and learned as much as we could about communication. We searched the word of God for His will regarding marriage. I grew to love marriage in a way I never knew before, and God birthed a ministry from our pain. God gave me a revelation, "Your pain is the currency of your purpose". Ultimately, I came to understand the pain we endure leads us to the problem we were created to solve. Too often, we discard our pain as fruitless, but it is the master key that typically unlocks our purpose.

Take Away Thought: *"Marriage was created to teach us to love unconditionally, forgive quickly and sacrifice selflessly".*

Chapter Thirteen:
PURPOSE & DESTINY

*A*ll my experiences, even up to this point have been necessary; they were intentional. They led me to my understanding of purpose. In 2012, I found the courage and strength to go back to school and get my first college degree. I attained what my father wanted most for me, a college- education. Ironically, that wasn't enough. I wanted more. I NEEDED to find the thing that I was created to do. I sought the problem I was created to solve! I believe everyone was created as a solution to a problem in the Earth.

When God created us, he created us solely as a solution. I had to dig deep and find what it is? What was it that I did so easily that gave me comfort...? What gave me peace during a horrible day, and how could I spread that peace? I had to know, why God created me; this was one of the most important questions I ever asked God. I was in search of more.

Our relationship with God and each other matured immensely. Everything we did regarding our marriage from this point was intentionally strategic (from sex to casual conversations, to how often we attended church– EVERYTHING)! We had already committed to the church where God led us. We had our family, and we were continually growing in the things of God. Gratefully, my husband's business grew rapidly as well... our lives were progressive but there was still a missing piece. There was still something that didn't quite connect.

I needed more for my life and so I dug deep into myself in search of me... in search of my divinely established purpose. I asked God, why am I here? Why did you save me from the pit? Why did you preserve me? Why did you keep me? Why? Why? God spoke so clearly...He said, "You are my joy. You are my encouragement to the world."

This was one of the most empowering things that I have ever experienced... to hear God tell me why he created me. He spoke to me in Jeremiah 1:5, God told me who I am.

There is no setup like a God-Setup! It propels the purpose of our lives and changes us for the rest of our lives! I didn't know how to do or what to do – in relation to what I needed to do. God spoke to me about being a life coach, and at the time I didn't know what a life coach was. I had never even heard of the term – "Life Coach!"

I was led to a gentleman, who travels the world as a life coach. His story is like mine; the light-bulb came on… the epiphany made me smile… I was called to use my voice in a way that would give God glory and bring hope and restoration to His people.

The gentlemen offered a Life Coach Certification course, and without any hesitation, I knew it was something I had to do. I knew this was my moment to unlock another door. I knew this was another piece to my puzzle, and it was very instrumental for me to become [my] purpose. Unquestionably, I took that course; my husband was so supportive, he spoke to me like the visionary he is! He helped me connect the pieces that I had failed to notice were already there! My husband, Samuel Gilmore made me realize I was already a life coach. I was already doing the thing that I was created to do. I just didn't know how to monetize it!

The Life Coach talked about how he took practical life experiences and turned them into lessons. He taught people how to overcome challenges in their lives. This was my light bulb again, but I didn't know how to step up. I didn't know how to step away from my past and allow my purpose to propel me to my future! I was challenged by self-defeating thoughts and personal sabotage. I questioned, "Is this a real job? Can I really do this?

After completing the course, I became my business. I was and am the product. I am the service. I didn't know what lied ahead of me. But I knew I had to take another step... I wanted to write a book; I had desired to do it for quite some time, but I didn't have the courage to do it, then.

When I took that course, my instructor said, "You have to write a book." That was my confirmation that the book had to happen, but I wasn't ready yet. I didn't have the confidence. God continued to work on me... I didn't understand how to utilize my past experiences of drug-usage, drug-dealing, bad relationships, and bad choices as inspiration for others. I realized it wasn't my experiences, but it was the fact that God brought me out of every one of them! That was the inspiration and the encouragement. Not that I was in them, but the fact that God brought me out of them. Who could deliver me from death time and time again… BUT GOD.

God lead me to Revelation 12:11 and it reads… "And they overcame by the blood of the lamb and by the words of their testimonies." I understood with complete clarity how important and valuable my testimony is; our testimonies are intentional and strategically intertwined into our lives by God… and in His infinite wisdom and power, He delivers us, so our testimonies can LITERALLY save someone else from the same detriment!

When I got this, when I understood this, I knew I could no longer hold my story! Liberation from my past would allow me to free someone else in the very near future! The only way I was going to get free was to tell it, I had to tell my story! My God had been too good, too merciful, and too loving for me to keep the power of my testimony SILENT! It was imperative for me to tell the masses what God had done for me!

The first time I spoke my testimony I was in a bible study. Without colorful euphemisms and deliberate omissions of the filthiness. I told my story – raw and unadulterated! I remember the flabbergasted looks on their faces. I didn't understand or discern what the shock was about, but they kept saying you don't look like what you've been through.

Their words encouraged me to tell another person, and another person, and the more people I told; the more liberated I BECAME. The more I glorified God and not my shame, the more I released the pain! Before I knew it, my liberation transformed into power, and my power transfigured into motivation, and the motivation is God's glory!

Purpose Fulfilled, Access Granted!!